DENVER
BRONCOS

STEVE POTTS

CREATIVE ❦ EDUCATION INC.

Published by Creative Education, Inc.
123 S. Broad Street, Mankato, Minnesota 56001

Designed by Rita Marshall

Cover illustration by Lance Hidy Associates

Photos by Allsport USA, Bettmann Archives, Diane
Johnson, Duomo, Photri, Sportschrome and Wide World
Photos

Library of Congress Cataloging-in-Publication Data

Potts, Steve.
    Denver Broncos/Steve Potts.
    p.   cm.
    ISBN 0-88682-365-X
    1. Denver Broncos (Football team)—History.   I. Title.
GV956.D37P68   1990
796.332'64'0978883—dc20   90-41254
                                            CIP

Denver, nestled in Colorado's Rocky Mountains, is one of America's most beautiful cities. In 1959 it had just about everything—stunning scenery, clean air, a booming economy. Everything, that is, except a professional football team. This changed in 1960, however, when the Denver Broncos were created.

Unfortunately, the team's appearance didn't contribute to the beautiful scenery. The Broncos, named after a 1920s Denver baseball team, were dressed in some of football's ugliest uniforms. Manager Dean Griffing, operating on a shoestring budget, had bought a set of horrible brown

A member of the first Bronco squad, Austin Gonsoulin.

jerseys and gold pants from the sponsors of the Copper Bowl, a college football bowl game which had gone bankrupt. Rounding out these eyesores were stockings with vertical brown and yellow stripes. The players complained and even offered to buy their own socks, but management wasn't listening.

It wasn't until 1962 that new coach Jack Faulkner decided the uniforms would have to go. After changing the team's colors to orange and blue, he announced the Great Sock Barbecue. Faulkner invited players and fans to a giant bonfire at the Broncos' practice field. The players, holding the hated socks above their heads, ran laps around the field. Then, to the cheers and howls of the fans, the players pranced around the fire, then tossed their old socks into the flames. The new, and better-dressed, Denver Broncos had been born.

1 9 6 0

Tight budget: The team couldn't afford playbooks— so quarterback Frank Tripucka diagrammed plays in the dirt.

FOOTBALL IN THE MILE HIGH CITY

The Great Sock Barbecue was one of the few things Denver fans had to cheer about during their team's first years. Football had returned to Denver in 1960 through the efforts of brothers Bob and Lee Howsam. Bob Howsam had joined Texas businessman Lamar Hunt in August 1959 to form the American Football League (AFL). Denver joined seven other teams in 1960 for the AFL's first season.

With only $400,000 budgeted for the young team, manager Dean Griffing had to scrimp and cut corners. The Broncos' first coach, Frank Filchock, was allowed to hire only two assistants. This small staff opened the team's first

Melvin Bratton carries a strong Denver tradition into the nineties.

*Jim Summers'
superb defensive
play was one of the
reasons Denver
boasted such a
tough defense.*

training camp at the Colorado School of Mines, where eighty players lived in one huge Army-style dormitory room.

Financial troubles were not Denver's only problems. Although the Broncos had a 7-7 record in 1962, every other year from 1960 to 1971 was a losing season. In fact, after the 1960 season ended, the Howsam brothers considered selling the team and moving it to another city. It took a major "Save the Broncos" campaign, and purchase by Denver businessmen Cal Kunz and Gerry Phipps in 1965, to keep the team in the Mile High City.

The Broncos' poor record in the early years certainly wasn't the fault of their fans or their home stadium. Broncos' fans set records for ticket sales beginning in 1965. After their new owners took charge, the Broncos asked their fans to "come out and support this team. After all, it's your own." This direct appeal worked. Since 1970, every Broncos' game in Denver has been sold out, a record many other teams would envy.

Fans also turned out to help the team improve its small stadium. Built in 1948 with seventeen thousand seats for baseball's Denver Bears, the stadium was too small to accommodate all the Broncos' fans. For the 1960 opening season, 17,700 new seats were added. When Denver voters turned down a bond issue to raise money to further improve the Broncos' home, the team's fans began a fund-raising drive in 1967. One year and $1.8 million later, the fund-raisers had remodeled and expanded the stadium, then turned it over to the city. Now named Mile High Stadium, it is the perfect place to catch the Broncos in action. Sixteen thousand new seats provided much more space for eager fans. Spectators helped to pass a $25 million bond issue in 1974 to enlarge the stadium again. Today it holds seventy-six thousand people.

Denver's fans have always cheered on their Bronco heroes, even when the team was losing. And it seemed in the early years that it lost a lot. Three of the fans' favorite Broncos during this period were Frank Tripucka, Lionel Taylor, and Floyd Little.

Frank Tripucka, an eleven-year veteran of pro football, was the Broncos' first quarterback. An alumnus of Notre Dame's famous Fighting Irish, Tripucka also acted as assistant coach. During the first year he had to diagram football plays in the dirt, because the team couldn't afford play books. Despite this handicap, Tripucka set team records for yards passed in a single game and touchdown passes in a single season.

Many of Tripucka's passes were sent spiraling to Lionel Taylor, who led the AFL in pass receptions in the years 1960 to 1963 and also 1965. The Broncos' career leader in number of receptions and receiving yardage, Taylor had been cut by the Chicago Bears. Thinking his playing days were over, he eagerly accepted an offer from the new Denver squad. Over the next seven years with the Broncos, Taylor was consistently ranked as one of the AFL's top receivers.

While Tripucka and Taylor provided the aerial fireworks, running back Floyd Little bolstered Denver's ground game. In all Little spent nine years (1967–1975) in a Broncos' uniform. As a halfback at Syracuse University, Little had rushed behind blocking by his friend, later Miami Dolphin great Larry Csonka. He had been a three

1 9 6 9

Floyd Little returned a punt for fifty-six yards to set up a victory over the Jets.

Like Frank Tripucka, John Elway is a talented quarterback. (pages 10–11)

time All-American in college. Little was the first round-one draft pick the Broncos had ever gotten. He was AFC rushing leader in 1970 and 1971, and the NFL's leader in 1971.

Despite fan support, stupendous efforts by team standouts, and superb coaching by Lou Saban, who had coached the Buffalo Bills to two AFL crowns, the Broncos ended 1971 with nine losing seasons behind them. It was time for a change.

1 9 7 4

Mr. Versatile: Jon Keyworth was a talented rusher, receiver and punt returner.

THE BRONCOS TURN AROUND

Change came to Denver in 1972 in the person of John Ralston, the Broncos' seventh head coach. Stanford University's former helmsman had led his team to two straight Rose Bowl victories. He intended to make the Broncos winners, too. "The goal here is to win the Super Bowl," he said at his first Denver press conference.

Ralston and Robert "Red" Miller, the coach who succeeded Ralston, led the Broncos to their first winning seasons in the club's history, including two AFC Western Division championships and an appearance in the 1978 Super Bowl. How did they do this? Much of the credit must rest with the coaches' boundless enthusiasm. As Red Miller said, "The Broncos will make Denver proud. We're not scared of anyone. We can beat any team, and we won't stop trying until the final gun sounds." Denver coaches also had what seemed like an endless supply of superstars to choose from to build a strong new team.

Jim Turner ended an already successful sixteen-year pro career with an eight-year stint in Denver (1971–1979). Out of 488 attempted kicks, Turner scored 304 career field goals, making him one of pro football's most successful kickers; he ranks third on the NFL's all-time career list. A quarterback during his college days at Utah State, he also played tight end and running back before becoming a pro placekicker. Teammates often remarked that Turner could do just about anything.

Lyle Alzado was a defensive end drafted out of tiny Yankton College in South Dakota in 1971. There was nothing tiny about Alzado, though. A large, powerful defenseman, Alzado also had been an amateur boxer with an impressive record: 33 straight wins, 22 of them with knockouts. An active worker in Denver charities, Alzado won the NFL's coveted Byron "Whizzer" White Award as the NFL Player Association's Man of the Year. Alzado seemed a strange man to like flowers, but he and his mother ran a flower shop in the off-season.

1 9 7 5

Top rusher! Running back Otis Armstrong was Denver's leading ground gainer.

Haven Moses, traded to Denver from the Buffalo Bills in 1972, became one of the game's finest wide receivers. A Bills' first-round draft pick in 1968, the talented San Diego State graduate had never reached his full potential with the ailing Bills. He did at Denver. Moses is still tied with Lionel Taylor for the most Broncos' touchdown receptions. He also ranks among the leading Broncos in number of receptions and yardage received.

Denver was quarterbacked in its winning seasons by Charley Johnson (1972–1975) and Craig Morton (1977–1982). Johnson came to Denver in 1972 through a trade with Houston. Although he was frequently injured during his pro career, he led the Broncos in passing—over one thousand seven hundred yards per year—for three years. His successes, noted Coach Ralston, made him "probably the finest natural leader I've ever met, on or off the field."

Craig Morton joined the Broncos in 1977 when Coach

13

1 9 7 7

Safety Bill Thompson and teammates snatched seven interceptions in a upset victory over Oakland.

Miller went looking for someone with a strong arm to stiffen up his offensive attack. Morton already had a decade of experience with the Dallas Cowboys and the New York Giants, but no one was really sure what he could do as a starter. At Dallas he had played backup to Don Meredith and Roger Staubach, men who needed little backing up. With the spotlight now on him, Morton rose to the occasion. He took the field, directed the offense, and led his team to six straight victories in the 1977 season.

Morton was aided in his efforts by a steamrolling defensive line that allowed few points against the Broncos. Known as the "Orange Crush," they slowed, stopped, and plowed under most of their opponents. Broncos' defensive coach Stan Jones had given them their name; as he held up a Broncos' home jersey in the locker room one day, he said, "From now on, our defense is going to be called the Orange Crush." Spurred on by this enthusiasm the fans, anxious to see their team in the playoffs, got a severe case of "Broncomania." Soon, the jerseys on the field were not the only things that were orange; orange bumperstickers, shoes, hats, pants, and banners filled the stands at each home game.

All of this fan support grew even stronger when the Broncos beat Pittsburgh 34-21 to reach the AFC championship game, where they would be pitted against the defending Super Bowl champion Oakland Raiders. The Broncos met the Raiders on New Year's Day in 1978 in cold Mile High Stadium. The game turned out to be one of football's most exciting playoff contests.

An even match between a strong Oakland offense and Denver's Orange Crush defense, the game began with two

Bronco wide receiver Ricky Nattiel.

Rick Upchurch's sixty-seven yard kickoff return provided one of Denver's few Super Bowl highlights.

long drives up the field by the Raiders. The Broncos' defense held, forcing Oakland to try two field goals. Only one kick made it through the uprights. Two plays later Craig Morton lofted a seventy-four-yard pass to Haven Moses. Moses caught it and ran it in for a touchdown. Jim Turner added the extra point for a 7-3 Denver lead. No one scored during the second period.

In the third quarter nerves grew tense. A fumble and Denver recovery put the Broncos in scoring position on the Oakland seventeen-yard line. Immediately Craig Morton passed to tight end Riley Odoms for a first down on the two-yard line. On the next play, Morton handed the ball to running back Rob Lytle. Lytle was grounded by Raider safety Jack Tatum's bone-crushing tackle and dropped the ball. Oakland's Mike McCoy jumped on the fumble.

But wait; the referee hadn't seen the fumble! He ruled that Lytle had been tackled and that the ball belonged to Denver. Tempers blew. One furious Oakland player pushed a referee. Socked with a penalty, Oakland was forced to put the ball on its one-yard line. Moments later Morton ran to the right side and passed to John Keyworth. He scored. "Go!Go!" Morton yelled. "Let's get another one and put this game away." The angry Raiders scored fourteen points in the fourth quarter, nearly clinching a victory, but Denver held on and came back with another touchdown to win 20-17. Morton had passed for 217 yards and the Orange Crush had held Oakland to only ninety-one yards rushing. A happy Broncos' team swarmed off the field as the sullen Raiders stomped to their locker room.

Although the Broncos lost in their first Super Bowl, beaten 27-10 by Dallas, things were looking up for the

Barefoot kicker Rich Karlis played for Denver in the 1980s. (page 17).

Karl Mecklenburg led the Orange Crush in the 1990s. (pages 18–19)   17

Rally time! Craig Morton brought Denver back from a twenty-four point deficit to defeat Seattle.

energized team. Coach Miller was proud of his players. "Listen," he said, "You don't have anything to be ashamed of. I'm forever proud of you. We'll come here again." Coach Miller, Craig Morton, and the Orange Crush put themselves in the AFC playoffs again in 1978 and 1979. Although they did not win these games, they cemented Denver's reputation as a combative, successful team, and they prepared Denver for their team's greatest years, the 1980s.

THE BRONCOS' STAMPEDE

After a 1980 season that ended in an 8-8 record, Red Miller left the Broncos to be replaced by the man who became the club's most successful coach: Dan Reeves. When he took over the Broncos in 1981, Reeves may have been the NFL's youngest coach, but he was certainly not lacking in experience.

Reeves had played for the Dallas Cowboys during their glory years, 1965 to 1972, as a running back. From 1970 to 1980 he was also one of the Cowboys' coaches, becoming one of the first NFL players who had dual player-coach roles. After participating in three NFC championship games, he went on to play or coach in seven Super Bowls (1966, 1967, 1970, and 1979 with Dallas and 1986, 1987, and 1989 with Denver).

As the Bronco head coach Reeves inherited an aging, injury-ridden team in 1981, but he quickly set about the task of signing on new talent. One addition was place-kicker Rich Karlis, who joined the team as a free agent in 1982. His soccer-style barefoot kicks made him one of the Broncos' top scorers. For four seasons he topped one hundred points and had one of the NFL's best career field goal percentages—nearly 70 percent. Often the difference between winning and losing, his kicks made the Broncos one of football's top-scoring teams.

Another key addition was Mike Harden, who often alternated between the safety and cornerback positions. As the mainstay of the Bronco defensive backfield Harden had five straight seasons as the Broncos' pass interception leader. As active off the field as on the turf, Harden owned a restaurant, attended law school, and worked with community youth projects in the off-season. As one Denver fan recently said, "Mike is really a good role model for kids, and a credit to his team."

1 9 8 2

Kicker Rich Karlis emerged from a 478-player free agent camp to win the starting job.

Reeves was also instrumental in improving the Broncos' running game. One big step toward improvement was made in 1982 when fifth-round draft pick Sammy Winder came to Denver. Holder of school records at Southern Mississippi in rushing attempts, points, and rushing touchdowns, he was one of his team's most dangerous offensive threats. Today, he is second on the list of the Broncos' all-time leading rushers and is tied for third in total touchdowns.

A trio of wide receivers known as the "Three Amigos" —Vance Johnson, Ricky Nattiel, and Mark Jackson— rounded out the Denver offense and bolstered the team's passing and scoring stats. Johnson, at 5'11" and 185 pounds is one of football's smallest receivers. He came to Denver after a shining career at Arizona. Also a long jumper in college, Johnson missed being on the 1984 United States Olympic team by a hair. "It was less than a quarter of an inch," Johnson mused sadly. "It broke my heart." A successful commercial artist, he had several

Quarterback John Elway and running back Andrew Lang.

showings in Denver galleries. "I don't go out and party," Johnson said, to dispel rumors about football players. "I like to be at home and paint. That's the image I want to portray, and it's a good one for the kids."

Even though Mark Jackson spent four weeks on injured reserve in 1988, he set personal single-season records in touchdowns, receptions, and yardage gained. Known for his speed and heart-stopping catches, third amigo Ricky Nattiel was Denver's first round draft pick in 1987. Nattiel, a college All-American, was also a leading league punt returner in 1988.

Perennial All-Pro linebacker Karl Mecklenburg was drafted out of the University of Minnesota.

While Reeves designed a finely tuned offensive-defensive mix, using such standouts as tight end Doug Cosbie, center Billy Bryan, and linebackers Tom Jackson and Karl Mecklinburg, his greatest accomplishment was in setting up a passing game that allowed two great quarterbacks, Craig Morton and John Elway, to raise the Broncos to Super Bowl heights again. When Reeves joined the team in 1981, Morton was about to begin his last year in the game. Many fans and fellow players thought Morton's weak knees wouldn't hold up to another season of battering. Reeves, however, had played with Morton in Dallas and knew what his former teammate was capable of. Reeves gave Morton the starter's job, and Morton didn't let his coach down. Even though the team failed to make the playoffs in 1981, it compiled a winning 10-6 record during Reeves's first and Morton's last year.

A disastrous 1982 season led Reeves to look for a new quarterback in 1983. The Broncos had put lots of time and effort into obtaining Purdue's Mark Hermann in 1981. But along with first-round draft picks for 1983 and 1984, Hermann was traded to Baltimore. Who were the Broncos so

24   *Clockwise: Steve Atwater, Bobby Humphrey, Dennis Smith, Ricky Nattiel.*

eager to get? None other than John Elway, a man many sportswriters called one of the "new breed" of winning quarterbacks.

While growing up in California, John Elway played both baseball and football in high school. His father Jack, football coach at Cal State Northridge, Stanford University, and later San Jose State, hoped his son would decide to play college football. John wasn't sure what to do. After leading his high school to the Los Angeles City Championship in baseball, Elway was chosen by the Kansas City Royals in their 1979 summer draft. But the Royals were too late. Stanford University head coach Ron Dowhower, a former Denver Broncos' assistant coach, had already signed Elway to play football at Stanford.

1 9 8 6

Strong safety Dennis Smith was named to the AFC's Pro Bowl team.

Before his first year of play at Stanford, Elway had already attracted attention for his prowess on the playing field. Steve Dils and Jim Plunkett, former Stanford star quarterbacks, returned to their alma mater to practice with the team during summer training camp. They and coach Dowhower recognized what an unusually accurate arm the young freshman had. Elway also could read plays well and already knew more of the playbook than many pro players. Although he wasn't used much his first year, Elway was the first sophomore All-American since 1963. An All-American in his junior and senior years, too, he was second in Heisman Trophy balloting in 1983. Holder of five major NCAA football records, Elway would be a prime draft choice in 1983.

Elway had a problem, however. He didn't want to play for the Baltimore Colts, the team that would get him in the draft. His fiancée Janet and his family lived on the West Coast, and he wanted to play for a West Coast team. When

1989 number 1 draft pick, Bobby Humphrey (#26). (pages 26–27)

*Mark Jackson (#80)
played a big part in
Denver's march to
the Super Bowl.*

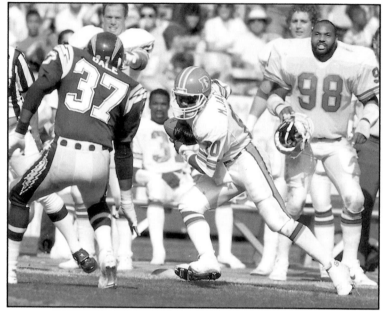

Baltimore refused to budge, Elway announced that "right
now, it looks like I'll be playing baseball with the New
York Yankees." He had played with their Oneonta, New
York farm club in 1982, the summer between his junior
and senior years at Stanford. Although Elway wasn't sure
how good he really was, the Yankees were willing to sign
him. He was the first number-one draft pick in college
football to ever refuse the draft.

Baltimore finally relented and traded his rights to the
Broncos. On May 2, 1983, John Elway signed a five-year $5
million contract with Denver. As the league's highest-paid
rookie, he was under immense pressure his first year. As
one sportswriter put it, everyone lined up to see "Elway-
mania" in action. In his first five games, the pressure got
the best of him. Elway started and three of the games were
Denver losses. Critics wondered if Denver's owners had

Elway's favorite target, Vance Johnson (#82).

Defensive back Mike Harden (#31).

The hard-hitting Steve Atwater.

Bronco quarterback John Elway continued to be one of the NFL's top signal-callers.

been "had" in their deal, especially when Steve DeBerg, the Broncos' experienced quarterback, came off the bench and won five of the next seven games. Elway's weeks on the bench helped, however. He came back to lead the team to victories over Cleveland and Baltimore, giving the Broncos a 9-7 record and winning them a play-off spot.

Behind a powerhouse defense and finely honed coaching, John Elway has led his team to four division and three AFC championships since 1984. In six short seasons he has set numerous Bronco career passing records. In 1988 he became the first NFL player to have four consecutive seasons with over three thousand yards passing and two hundred yards rushing. But even more impressive is the fact that in five seasons (1983–1988), Elway has directed his Broncos to more season and overall wins than any other league quarterback.

What Elway, Reeves, and the Broncos have not been able to do is win the Super Bowl. Although the team reached the Super Bowl in 1986, 1987, and 1989, it lost all three games (in 1986, 39-20 to the New York Giants; in 1987, 42-10 to the Washington Redskins; and in 1989, 55-10 to the San Francisco 49ers). In spite of all that talent, a team younger than most, and a group of dedicated coaches, that little something extra has been missing. If it is found, however, look for Denver to be a strong threat to finally claim a Super Bowl victory in the 1990s.